Contents

Dedication

I am dedicating this book to my eldest sister Iris Ann Johnstone (nee hall), who died on the 15th of December 2021 after a battle with cancer. Iris could seem bossy at times with her overpowering personality. She would do anything to help anyone out whenever possible, friends and family alike. She devoted her life to her husband Bob and her two sons, Sean and Craig. Iris spent many hours and days babysitting and childminding her beloved grandchildren. She worked hard all her life. After starting as a qualified hairdresser, Iris went on to work at the shoe-store in the old Redhill Co-op. From there she went on to work at Foxboro-Yoxalls and then after starting her family, she did care work. Iris finished her working life as a part time assistant at Batchelor Collingwood in Horley which was a very prestigious store.

Our family and friends will always remember her with pride and adoration.

Foreword

I can't quite remember how long I've known Alan. Probably only eleven or twelve years at most, nevertheless, he is one of those characters you feel you have known all your life.

We first met when I was working as a bar tender at The Garland pub in Redhill. Back then he was a regular evening shift visitor, more often than not having been out. and about somewhere during the day and usually accompanied by his good friend John (A.K.A Captain). The Garland was often their last stop off before heading home for the night and Al would regularly share the day's adventures over a pint or two of Harvey's. It's probably no surprise that Alan is a dedicated real ale enthusiast and a loyal supporter of many neighbourhood watering holes. I think it's fair to say there's nothing he likes more than a decent pint and good company.

Some years down the road and I work in a different Redhill local (The Garibaldi Community Pub) but apart from that nothing much has changed. Besides being a little less nimble on his feet, Alan certainly hasn't. We still catch up a few times a week and at 74 he is as sharp as a new pin with the mischievous streak of an eleven-year-old boy. In short (no pun intended) Al' is a pint-sized Chap with a huge personality. He has a boyish sense of humour but has little patience with 'morons" - a word I have heard him use frequently to describe various people over the years. He is certainly never shy about speaking his mind! He loves to read, does the crossword a couple of times a week and, oh yes, he likes to yodel from time to time too. He has always been extremely proud of his mathematical prowess, even a tad big headed at times if I'm honest!

Alan has done quite a lot and gotten about a bit during his life, and he enjoys talking about it. He has always wanted to write a book and I'm delighted that he has now achieved his dream. An easy read with a beer in the evening, I hope you enjoy this nostalgic journey through a scrapbook of memories as much as I have. I'm sure there will be more adventures and stories to come, and I hope we continue to share them at the bar (one side or another) for many years to come.

 Jane B

P.s Alan, you owe me a beer ! x

Chapter One: "Captain Macca"

This is an autobiography, but I don't want it to be just about me. It is a book about the things and the people I that I have loved and respected. Things like football and people like John McBride.

I started playing football at the age of twenty-two or twenty-three, with a team called Eastern Sports. We were named this due to the fact that the group who formed the team drank in the Southeastern Pub opposite the Redhill train station. Later we would meet in other pubs like the Tower and the George and the Dragon, but it started in the Southeastern.

We played our games on 'The Ring', a piece of ground that stretched from Redhill Common down to the Plough pub. It was a bit rough and ready, with nowhere to change or even a proper pitch, but we made do for a few years. (There was a changing room but it was just a wooden shack with a padlock)

There was a local company that made paints named Johnston who sponsored a local team and a backup reserve side. This reserve team shut down and we were given the chance to take over, as long as we renamed ourselves 'Johnston Sports

Reserves'. We were offered a pitch at Brockham in Betchworth, on a part called the Big Field, which consisted of several 'rugby four' football pitches. The team had a good ground, luxurious changing facilities and a clubhouse to boot. We had fallen on our feet!

Report in the local paper about our new football team, of the seven names mentioned only three are still with us. Myself, Tony Hazelgrove, and Brian Lambert.

The lads who played lived on Colesmead Road, Southmead, Northmead, Gatton Park and went to Frenches and Redstone Hill School. There was the star player David Foot, he was mustard, but if he tried to go past me, he ended up on his back! Johnny Bagely, known as Bags and Terry Pope. There were two sets of brothers the Dibbles, Paul and Roger. And the Sladkowski's, Micky and Steve. The latter was the goalkeeper, but when he couldn't make a game, Andy Brewer, a big fellow, would play instead. He wasn't much of an outfield player but in later life managed amateur clubs so he must have had something about him football wise. There was Micky Hutchins and his old man. Micky and his mum were both Chelsea supporters and Tony Hazelgrove, a work a day footballer who eventually became our manager and Paul Roberts who became the secretary. Like me these guys weren't the best players on the pitch. I was small and fast but that was about it! Due to this I took on other vital tasks such as being the regular linesman and reluctantly the club treasurer. I was coerced into doing this because no-one else would do it, and in those days your club would be fined if you didn't have one. Getting subs out of this lot was hard work but if they didn't want to pay and they were any good then they normally got away with it. But I still got the same respect as the players.

"Johnston Sports" came second in Redhill and District league Division One that year. At our presentation night I was awarded a plaque which was the same as the players', except with the word 'Treasurer' engraved beneath.

The trophy that the football team clubbed together and presented to me in 1980 lovely gesture. Thanks boys!

But the person I really want to talk about was John McBride, the Captain. Or 'Macca' as we knew him. Macca was a well-known Redhill lad who lived for football and was very good at it. He could play in any position on the field, goalkeeper, defensive sweeper, midfield or forward line. And over the years he played for many local teams apart from Johnston Sports.

Macca taught me the offside rules of football and was always shouting at me and gesticulating at me while I was doing my linesman duties! He called me" Ally boy" but I didn't argue. He was a big fellow with a strong athletic physique. Macca worked as a council dustman and built up his muscles doing so (unlike me who worked as a postman for thirty years...) The McBride's were a large family of five brothers and three sisters. In fact, Macca was actually the illegitimate son of one of the sisters and a Polish soldier and was raised by his grandparents, who I only knew as Jock and Mrs. McBride. The family was feared on the Northmead as a hard clan. But John was gentler, even though he was a tall strapping lad. I met him because in those times you met everyone! On the council estates everyone knew each other's names. It was a different time! Our captain honed his football skills on the Colesmead Recreation Park, opposite where I lived on the Colesmead road. I have many happy memories of the 'Rec' as it was the scene of many soccer, cricket and other the games that boys and girls play.

A lot of local people probably didn't know that Macca had broken his legs on two separate occasions. The first time was on the back of a motorbike owned by a friend of his called Colin Wales in a minor accident. The second time was during a knockabout game on the Rec, in a tackle with another lad called Ron Bachus. I witnessed the incident, as I was also playing in the match. There a loud clicking sound but I thought nothing of it. The next thing I know the lads were crowded around him, an ambulance arrived and off he goes to hospital. This was the second time he had broken that leg. So, it was almost a miracle that he became such a good footballer. But Macca was a man's man. He liked his beer, a fag or two and the ladies. He had an engaging sense of humour and wit. Anyone could be on the end of his jokes and cracks, including yours truly!

I remember one Saturday afternoon (it was the summer break, so there was no league football to be played), a small gang of us took the train to Brighton. Myself, Micky Slad, Ron Lambert, Tony Hazelgrove and Macca. I was wearing a railwayman's hat, which was given to me by a station porter at Redhill during the days that I loaded and unloaded mail bags there. We were all walking down towards the sea front when all of a sudden Macca sneaks up behind me, snatches my hat, plonked it on his own barnet and runs off. About half hour later, one of the lads informs me that Macca has been arrested by local policemen for impersonating a railway officer.

"Ha serves you right. I liked that hat!" I said.

After his release Macca is given a summons to appear in court, found guilty and given a fiscal punishment. Some days later in the pub, Macca walks up to me.

"You ought to pay half my fine", he said.

"You should buy me another hat! " I replied.

Cheeky sod! I thought. Getting money out of a treasurer's like getting blood out of a stone! This one of Macca's many pranks certainly backfired on him.

All the events I have related to took place during the late sixties, seventies and early eighties, after which time I had resigned my position of club treasurer on good terms with everyone, to concentrate on playing bar billiards. It was probably a sign of me getting a little older and the start of my tendency towards my social imbibing life.

I had worked as a welder at BLS, British Industrial Sand. The company used to make bricks; in fact the Brickmakers Arms pub in Redhill got its name from the works. After that I worked as a Postman. Unfortunately I had a stroke when I was fifty, and the Post Office forced me to leave. I had to fight for my pension, but a chat with a union representative and a doctor soon sorted that out.

Macca's life took a different path. He carried on playing football for a while and even got scouted by Crystal Palace. Unfortunately, Macca could be his own worst enemy. As a kid he would swear a lot, and this carried on during his football career. More often than not Macca would be sent off for using bad language and this was ended up being the reason that his trials at Crystal Palace ended. It was a shame because Macca, had a great football brain and he was the only one who did in the family as his brothers never played the game. He carried on with the sport though and played in goal for Redhill F.C. Macca carried on working as a dustman and married a girl called Sue.

They moved to Merstham near a pub called the Iron Horse and had three sons together.

And they lived happily there until the June 2002. When John McBride's life came to a tragic end.

I was on holiday in Cornwall and Devon during this time, arriving home on Saturday 22nd of June. The day after I received a phone call from my sister, Val, to tell me that Macca had drowned in the Thames River the week before. I was shocked, gobsmacked, to say the least. At the time everyone had World Cup football fever. The England team were attempting to repeat the heroics of the1966 tournament. Fat chance of that!

I have often wondered how much this programme would fetch on the market. It won't be sold until I'm brown bread! Priceless memory!

Macca was staying at his son Paul's place at Teddington lock, which backed on to the Thames. England had managed to beat

Denmark 3-0 and had made it into the quarter finals. It had been a while since we had done so well in the World Cup and so Macca and a couple of other guys decided to celebrate by swimming across the river! Sadly, they misjudged how strong the currents were and were swept away before managing to reach the opposite bank. Macca's two friends managed to survive, but our Captain's body was found downstream sometime later.

I'll never forget John McBride as he was one of my idols. He lived for his football, and sadly, died for the love of it!

Footnote

About three years prior to forming Eastern sports F.C., the Monson Road club formed a team which I signed up with and played for, mostly as a reserve player.

I became their first treasurer. (What is it about me that people trust to look after their finances? Must be my algebra qualification !). We played at the "Ring" down from the Plough pub. When we started our team at the South Eastern, I resigned my post both as treasurer and player. I remained good friends with the Monson Road players, and the two teams had a good rapport. During my visits to the club at Sunday lunchtimes, we often had a star footballer in for a drink by the name of Derek Pessee. He played for Millwall and Crystal Palace and his brother Mick lived in Lyndale road where the Monson club is situated. Mick was a P.H.G at Redhill post office, so I knew him quite well. About three years ago, I was in the Sun pub in Redhill when I noticed someone staring at me.

"Don't you remember me?" he said.

I did not.

"You used to call me Bobby." he said.

It was Derek Smalley from South Mead, from when we played football out on the Rec. He styled himself in the mould of Bobby Moore, obviously not quite as good but he played for the Monson team and others. He was in the pub with Alun Thomas and celebrating his daughter Shonda's fiftieth birthday party. There were several people who played for Monson F.C. all those years ago, including Wally Stevenson, who sadly died recently. But it was happy re-union, a pleasant surprise and a reminder of my footballing days.

Chapter Two: School Days

I'll begin with a brief history of my childhood and teens through to my twenties.

I was born in East Surrey hospital situated in Shrewsbury Road on 8th August 1947, a year before the NHS (National Health Service) came into existence. My mother was named Lil and my father Dennis. I was their first son, them having my sisters, Iris, four years before and Val two years previously. They named me Alan, no middle name necessary. We lived in Monson Road until I was a year old and then we were rehoused by the council in Colesmead road the recreation ground I mentioned in the previous chapter.

Around this time, I became ill with pneumonia and as you can tell, survived. It became clear later when I started school that I had hearing problems as both teachers and pupils noticed that I was not responding to them. It became clear that I was completely deaf in the left ear and only had partial hearing in the right. As this was only noticed at school, I will never be sure whether this affliction was from my illness or whether I was born with the problem. Like Buddy Holly sang, I guess it doesn't matter anymore! I attended Frenches primary school from the age of 5 years old and this was an exciting time for me. Nineteen fifty-three was the Coronation year and there were celebrations across the country, including the parties and games on my beloved Colesmead recreation ground. It's amazing to think of the Queen back then, especially considering her 'Maj' is still with us at the age of 95.

From the age of eight I attended Merstham middle school. Charlie Agate was the headmaster at the time, and he was liked and respected by pupils and teachers in equal measure. Charlie had a very likeable personality, and it was easy to see why people enjoyed engaging with him. At eleven I proceeded to Frenches secondary school. At first, I found this place a little scary. It was not exactly "Hogwarts" but it looked frightening to the boy I was back then. My two previous schools were both single storey buildings but Frenches has two floors with a science lab that looked like something out of the movies. The deputy head was even named Mr. Fright! Although the headmaster was called by the much less sinister name of Mr. Grant.

Mr. Grant would hold assembly meetings in the main hall and would always be attired in his mortarboard and black shiny cloak, so maybe it was more like Hogwarts than I thought! When he was around there was a deathly hush, such was his presence, he was a wizard when it came to algebra and his skills at teaching the subject were just as magical. His mentoring meant that I passed the college of preceptor's certificate in Algebra.

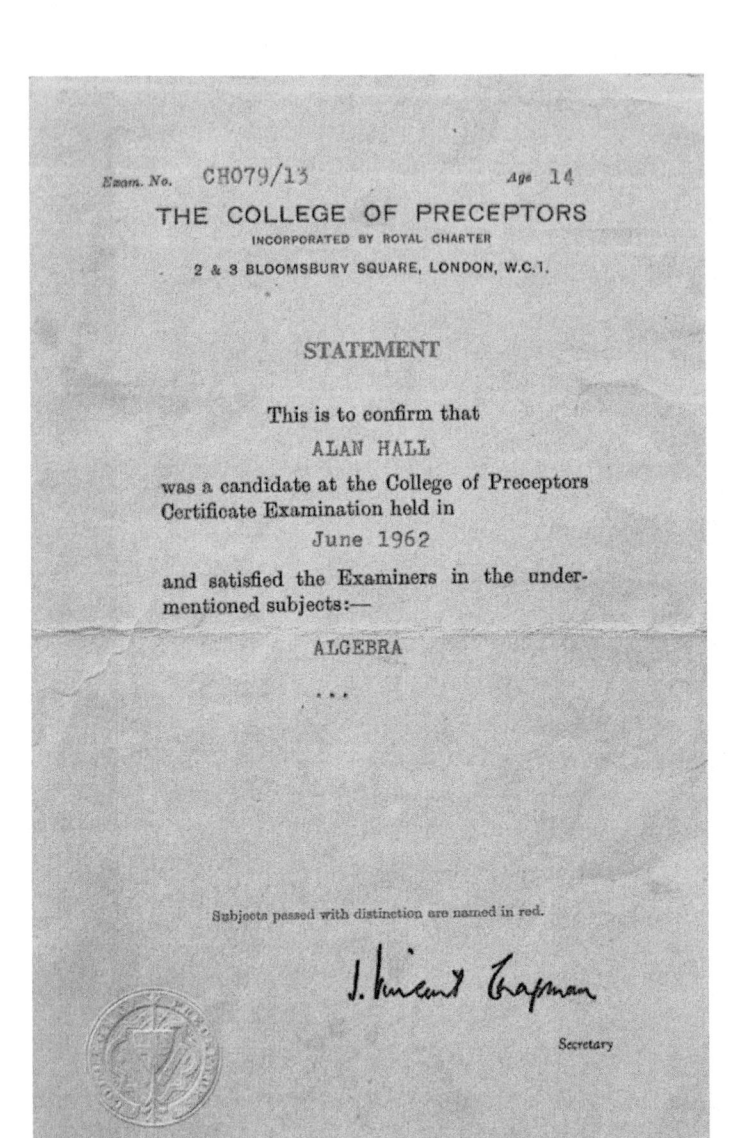

My algebra pass in the last year of school. An indicator of my financial knowledge.

As for Mr. Fright, well for some of the schoolboys he certainly lived up to his name. He cut an imposing figure and was very strict in class but generally a fair man in my opinion! Occasionally pupils from other classes were brought to him for a rollicking, acting as headmaster in Mr. Grant's absence. You could see these boys cowering with fear! On one occasion I was ordered out of class for upsetting the history teacher. This humourless man glowered at us all, asking why we were sitting around like sacks of potatoes. I stood up and said, "excuse me sir, would that be King Edwards?"

"Out! get out!" he shouted out at me, as I stood along the corridor, waiting to be called back in. Mr Fright arrived, and on seeing me, asked why I was standing outside classroom. I told him I was ordered out for laughing.

Fright looked at me and said "You are still laughing now you little so-and-so" he walked away shaking his head and I swear I could hear him chuckling!

Fright was my house- master for about two years and I got on ok with him. He taught English, and Mathematics. I say Maths but instead of the dry stuff Fright would talk more about finance, explaining how Government Fiscal Administration worked. How cool is that? I learned a lot from him.

The woodwork and metalwork huts for Frenches School were situated in Southmead, not far from where I lived. They were in the grounds I of Bishop Simpson's school for girls. These lessons usually took place on a Friday afternoon, which was often a nice finish to the school week for a young lad (wink, wink!). However, the metalwork teacher, a certain Mr. Perry, was not the nicest person in the world. One afternoon during a lesson I was at the water basin in the classroom. A couple of my school mates were outside and one of the lads asked me to throw out a wet rag. I didn't know why he wanted it, but I grabbed a cloth anyway. I soaked it under the tap and just for a laugh threw it in my friend's face. I turned around after this mischievous deed to be confronted by Mr. Perry He smashed the palm of his quite large hand across my face!

"You can fuck off home, and I will see the headmaster about this on Monday morning" Perry said as my head rang. But when Monday came, I was not summoned to the headmaster's office, and I feel sure that Mr. Grant would not have been happy to hear of this assault on my person. Could you imagine this kind of thing happening today without repercussion in this namby-pamby world now!?!

As the sixties arrive, my school days are about to come to an end.

"You're leaving school and getting a job to start paying your way," my mum says to me toward the end of nineteen sixty-two. In those days you didn't argue with your elders. I knocked on Mr. Grant's office door to tell him of the decision.

"I don't think you are quite mature enough to start work Alan", he said.

 "This is I one way of gaining maturity isn't sir!", I said.

So that was goodbye to Frenches secondary school and its eclectic cast of teachers and hello to the real world of work.

Chapter Three: How I became a Postman

My first job application was with Fuller's Earth, one of the biggest employers of Redhill. The interview did not go well. They looked at me as if to say, "who is this little squirt?" This feeling was correct as a week later I received a letter telling me that my services were not required.

 Boxing day 1962 begins the coldest winter in living memory with snowstorms and blizzards through to mid-March 1963. So, the first week of January found me tramping the pavements of Holmethorpe industrial estate through thick layers of snow and ice. I knocked on the doors of several factories and workshops looking for work, but it was to no avail. My last chance sat at the end of Holmethorpe avenue as the buildings of British industrial Sand Ltd. (B.I.S) came into sight.

 I tried the front office to be confronted by Uncle Don, my dad's eldest brother.

"What brings you here then Alan?" he said.

"I'm looking for a job Uncle Don".

The man rubbed his chin and gave me a smile.

"I suppose as the weather's so bad; I'll have to do an interview for you now," he said.

After the interview he booked me in as a trainee welder, starting the next Monday at 8am.

"Now, you will be working with a lot of older people, and some might be a little scary so don't be cheeky 'cos I know what your like" he said. Talk about sarcastic nepotism!

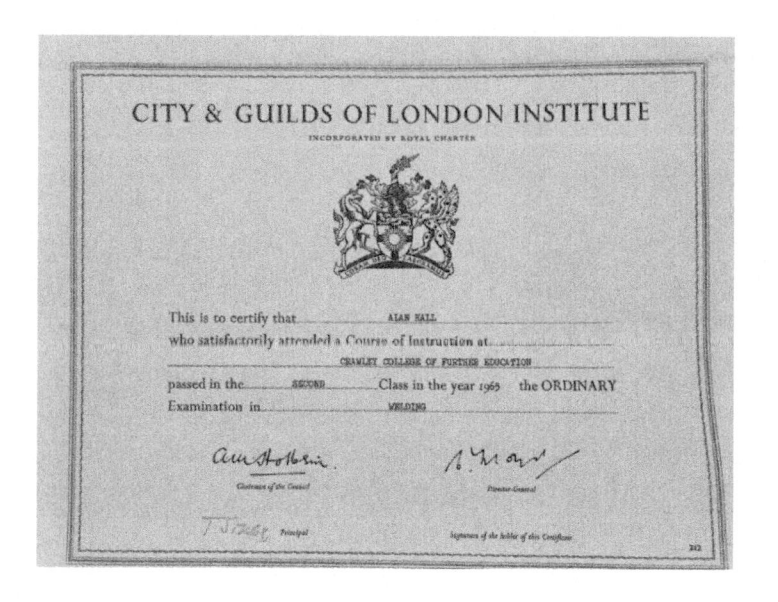

My welding certificate which I took at Crawley college of further education.

My Uncle Don died this year (April 2021), a month after his 101st birthday. He was a World War Two veteran and participated in the D Day landings. Don was married three times and outlived them all. He was a remarkable man.

Uncle Don in his military days

I worked for B.I.S. for over five years of mostly happy days. It a good company to work for with a social club unit that organised many trips and social events. One such treat was a trip to Stamford bridge which has stuck with me to this day as it is how I became a Chelsea supporter. On another B.I.S. sponsored do, we travelled to Wembley and saw the first world cup match of 1966, England v Uruguay. You probably remember that the original World Cup, the Jules Rimet cup, being stolen. It was eventually abandoned and found by a dog called Pickles, buried in someone's garden. I actually worked with Pickles owner, Dave Corbett, whilst working at the Post Office later on in life. He was a very comical man who bought a new house with the financial reward that Pickles earned him.

B.I.S social events also took us to professional boxing matches. One such match was a world title fight. It was Tuesday, 7* September in 1965 at the Earls Court arena. The bout was for the featherweight championship of the world. The competitors were Vicente Saldivar (Mexico) versus Howard Winstone (Wales). After the fifteen, three-minute rounds, the Welshman lost on a points decision.

Today (30 October 2021) as I'm reading my Daily Mirror, a newspaper I've stayed with all my life, I notice a photo of a Boris Johnson, the Prime Minister, making a bank card payment to the Royal British legion's centenary appeal. The recipient of this payment is army veteran Tom Dempsey aged eighty-four. This popular man was one of my first workmates at B.I.S and he was a top bloke. What a strange coincidence!

Tom Dempsey was one of my first workmates at B.I.S in 1963.

Sports meant a lot to me back then and I still have my programs for the boxing and world cup trips, and football matches at Stamford bridge and Crystal palace in the seventies.

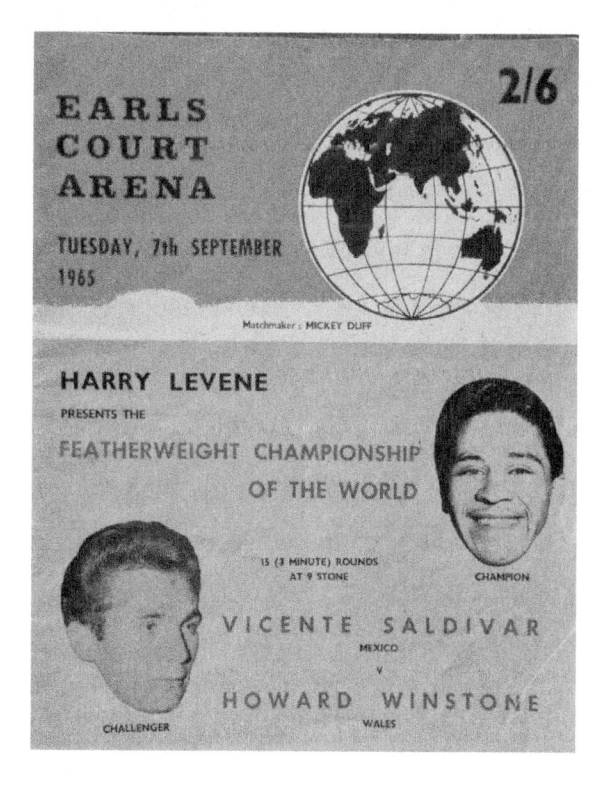

Boxing was a huge draw in those days. It no longer appeals to me as much.

The last two in particular meant a lot to me as they were with my good friend Brian Puplett who later became my brother in-law, marrying my younger sister Annette. Sadly, Brian died in 1991 at the age of forty-five from meningitis, a year older than me at the time. It was an age that was too young to die at and it was a sad loss to all his friends and relatives.

At the beginning of 1968 I was starting to get restless and felt I needed to move on from B.I.S. I was poached (head-hunted they call it today) by a Mr. Obid Rose from Southmead. He was the foreman at the workshop of the R. Smith company. It was down on the Balcombe Road in Horley, just up the road from the Kings Head pub which is still there to this day. The company made dumper trucks, scrapers and structures that involved steel construction. Here there was plenty of scope for me to use my welding abilities.

I made some good friends amongst my new colleagues, and again we organised some social activities, which included trips to the seaside in the summer and Christmas parties held in a hall in Horley in the winter.

I had a nickname at B.I.S. I was dubbed 'Pooney' which was actually supposed to imply I was 'puny'. But one of the perpetrators, my work mate John Madden had never learned to talk properly (he was what was known as a 'Merstham meathead'). At R. Smith my new 'good friends' gave me a new nickname. I became Albert due to my surname of Hall. How novel!

One day whilst I was working at R. Smith, an office worker from upstairs told us all to vacate the building.

"I say chaps there's a fire in our office" he said. We filed out to the car park that sat alongside the workshop. I decided to sit and inside my car, a Triumph Herald while we waited for some kind of announcement. Suddenly a fire engine appeared and came clanging into the yard. A few minutes later our manager, Mr. Potter told us that we can all go home. I didn't need asking twice. I turned the ignition key, and I was out like a shot!

Suffice to say the workshop did not burn down. About a week later we are all called back and were told that the company had been taken over by "Mattbro", a firm which ran a workshop across the road.

Staff from the two companies mixed together as no one was sacked, but right from the beginning, the works union life didn't feel the same. My feelings of doubt became a reality when the charge-hand, a bloke named Jack Marley, came marching through the workshop with a sheath of redundancy notices. He gave me mine with a huge grin on his face. Let's just say he was never a great friend of mine.

So, in Mid-November I became unemployed and had two miserable months on the dole. My redundancy money didn't last long due to lazy days in the pubs amongst other things. December 1971 consisted mostly of journeys to the job centre looking for work that wasn't there and signing on in the dole queue for my giro cheque every week. In those days it was humiliating not to be earning a crust, so I desperately wanted a job. One afternoon I'm reading the "Surrey mirror" and spotted an advert in the jobs section asking for applicants for postmen. I spoke to a guy I knew called Pip Sadler about the job. He had been a postman and driver for many years. He lived in Monson Road with his mum Queenie and was well known as a local piss-artist. He was also a well-known flatulent! Many a night he would stink the pubs out with his foul emissions from where the sun doesn't shine!

"Go for it Alan and if you don't like it, you can always leave and try your luck somewhere else", Pip said to me.

Incidentally Pip's son, David Sadler, played for our Johnstone sports team in defence. He was a very good player, but he never played for Man Utd. (He was too good for them!)

I applied for the job as postman and was interviewed in early January 1971 by the Chief Inspector, a Mr. Joe Pratt. There was a simple written test to check I could read and then a quick chat took place.

"Can you ride a bicycle" Joe said.

"Yes, but I will need one with a low saddle", I said.

"We can get a spanner to lower the saddle to suit your height, or lack of."

Monday, 10th January 1972 was my first day working for the Post Office, or Royal Mail, whichever you prefer to call it. From that day I spent thirty years, delivering mail and sorting, working on the rail station platforms, loading and unloading mail bags on the trains. Getting people's letters to them.

And that that is the story of how I became a postman.

Chapter Four: Brushes with the Law

The first incident I had with the law I can remember was pretty tame. I was cycling home from Merstham youth club (which was in Oakley Youth Club which was situated on Radstock Way) pedalling along Battlebridge lane. I spotted a foot patrol policeman, Dixon of dock green style for those that remember it. He steps out in front of me and orders me to stop.

He says, "do you realise your front light isn't on?"

I looked down, flicked the switch to no effect.

"The battery must have run out" I said. I looked at the rear light but that was ok, lit up with a nice red glow. So, with all the cheek of a sixteen-year-old, I said "back lights ok, so I should be able to ride the rest of the way".

Mr. Plod not amused!

"Do you come from a dopes school?" he said.

"No, I work for BIS, I might not be very big but I'm a working adult now."

With that Mr. plod says "get off your bike and you can walk the rest of the way and if I ever catch you up to mischief, I shall arrest you and take you to the police station"

I do as I'm told and push my bike around the corner and looks around to see Mr. Plod is out of sight. He is so I jump back in the saddle and I'm home within five minutes.

Talk about cocky teenagers !

My second brush with the law was slightly more serious. I was about a year older than when my last brush occurred at seventeen and seven months. I'd moved on from youth clubs and entered the brave new world of pubs!

On a Saturday evening around march April 1965, I entered the Tower pub in Redhill. In those days this pub had a saloon bar at the back and a public bar facing the main road. Adjoining the public bar was a little off- license. I've ordered a drink, a stout and cider, and sat down with Porky Wheatland, a BIS workmate of mine and his beloved

Betty. It was busy and music was being played by the residential organist on the stage with occasional guest singing from the customers. People were walking in and out of this bustling town pub and I wasn't taking much notice of who was coming in.

"Sit down Pooney" said Porky.

Before I realised the reason why I look around to see three uniformed policemen walking towards me. The middle one came over to me.

"Are you eighteen young man ?" he said.

"No, I'm seventeen and a half" I answered truthfully.

His notepad came out and he demanded my name, address and date of birth. With that, I'm ordered out of the pub with the manageress Eileen shouting at me.

"Don't come back you little swine" she said.

Talk about a humiliating experience ! But there's more to come.

The next Monday morning, I was back at work and it seems everyone has heard about my brush with the law. Of course, I got admonished from my peers, all taking the piss and full of guffaws. I must have had the reddest face in redhill that morning due to the embarrassment that everyone knew. A couple of weeks past and I've almost forgotten about this event when out of the blue a letter arrives. It is a police summons ordering me to appear in Reigate court. I had informed my foreman that I would be taking a day off, giving him a cock & bull story about an interview or something.

The day comes and I'm in the courthouse being questioned as to why I've committed this heinous crime.

"Saturday nights I get fed up watching telly or what not. I like to let my hair down and spend some of my hard-earned wages," I said.

"You must find other things to do and take up some hobbies or activities" the barrister replied.

I nearly said that pubs and drinking ales were my hobby but thought better of it!

The court bench retires behind the scenes to decide what kind of punishment fits the bill. No pun intended !

The law enforcers came back out into the court and informed me, and two other lads who were caught in other pubs, that a conditional discharge for only one year is served with not even a fine. I thought that was the end of all that, but more humiliation is to come. I will elaborate.

The following Friday I entered the workshop at BIS to loud cheers and laughing . I thought 'what's this all about then?' My charge-hand was there waiting with the Surrey Mirror a newspaper.

"You are on the front page, oh yes !" he said,

It was a report about my under-age drinking court case. I had the reddest face in Redhill again ! The chargehand Stan said

"You kept that bloody quiet, didn't you?" the chargehand Stan said.

"Yeah, but the bloody Surrey Mirror has blown all of that haven't they," I said. Talk about famous local notoriety. a badge of honour for life.

Months later on the 8th of august 1965 I reach the age of eighteen and was finally legally old enough to drink alcohol (heaven). I took a week's holiday for this momentous event and strolled down to Redhill town to have a beer in the Queens pub. (This place is now a Job Centre opposite the Wetherspoons "Sun" pub. What a disgrace) I was sitting on the steps of the Queens with a beer in my left hand, armed with my summons and birth certificate, waiting for a policeman to admonish me. Mr. Plod eventually walked by and didn't take a blind bit of notice of me. Oh dear! The cops must have some kind of intuition on these matters.

Just as well I suppose. They would probably find something else to hang on me.

My third brush with the law is slightly more serious and I'm not too proud of myself with regards to this incident I took driving lessons when I was about twenty in a Triumph Herald. I passed my test first time, and the driving test centre was in North Street, Redhill in those days. I was slightly shocked to pass on the first try. not because I thought I was not good enough, but because I had a bit of an argument with the stuffy examiner !

After my success I decided to buy my own car. You guessed it, I bought a Triumph Herald of my own. It was my pride and joy, and I did many trips to all sorts of places for holidays.

Me in my triumph herald (141 WPA) at about 21 years old. In the background is David Ongley who lived next door to our family.

I will get to the point now and describe how my car driving came to a sudden end. One Saturday afternoon I decided to drive to Bletchingly to visit Mick and Eileen Adams and their family. Eileen was my cousin, the daughter of my aunt Beatrice dad's elder stepsister. I loved it over there. The kids were friendly and there were dogs, cats and pet ferrets all over the place. It was mayhem but still relaxing.

After having something to eat and a drink, between 8 and 9 o'clock I drove towards Redhill and decide to go to the Monson Road club before going home. After a couple of pints of mild I decided to stay the rest of the evening and sup some more somewhat stronger bevvies. Big mistake. At closing time at the club, I got in my car and drove up Monson Road and along Gatton Park Road, then took a left at top of Colesmead road. I became distracted for some unknown reason and took my eyes off the road. The next moment there was a 'crunch crash' and my head banged into the windscreen. I looked up to see that I had crashed into the back of a stationary van. I reversed back to view the damage and surprisingly there were just mere scratches. There was nobody about, so I drove home, deciding that I would go up to this house to apologise the next morning and exchange insurance details if necessary.

Outside my parent's house I got out of my car to check any damage to my Triumph Herald . Oh dear! There was a big wedge in the bonnet and water leaking from the radiator onto the road. As I'm examining the damage. I'm suddenly surrounded by different neighbours and mates from all parts of Colesmead road. Also among them was the owner of the van I had pranged into the night before. I apologised to this man and said that we can sort out the insurance issues the following morning. He seemed quite happy with this arrangement, and I had every intention of complying with it. However his wife, who was also there, wasn't.

"Someone call the police, he's not getting away with this," she screamed into the crowd.

Among this group of people was my mate Micky s l from Southmead.

"Come round to my house and I'll make you a cup of coffee. You look a bit spaced out," he said.

Indeed, I was! We went to Mick's parent's house and coffee is brewed and drunk in the kitchen. After having a chat between us it's decided that I stay the night in the garage with a blanket wrapped round me under the bonnet of his dad's car. I soon fell asleep and woke up next morning feeling disorientated and rather groggy, wondering where the hell I am. Then it all came back to me and I realised what a mess I'd got myself into!

I got up from under the car, folded up the blanket and took it into the kitchen. I decided to walk home and go to bed for a proper sleep. When I eventually woke up and went for breakfast, I'm given a rollocking from my mum (deservedly so to). I decided to walk up the road to talk to the owner of the van. He didn't seem too worried since there were just a couple of scratches. From there I walked to the police station to report the accident. The duty constable took some notes, asked some questions etc. and then dismissed me from the station. After that I carried on as normal, wondering what would happen next. for the next couple of weeks, the neighbours and people round the Monson club would talk about nothing else (talk about soap operas!)

My car was inspected by the insurance reps, and they decided it was a write-off sometime after that I received a cheque because I had a fully comprehensive insurance policy. Sometime after this I'd almost put it all behind me and was relieved. But then I received a summons from the police charging me with "failing to stop at the scene of an accident". I found myself back in court again, about four and half years after my underage drinking incident. I report to the authorities giving my name and particulars and the clerk over his glasses at me.

"I assume you are pleading guilty" he said.

"No, I am not. I'm pleading innocent," I replied.

"Who is your solicitor?" he asked.

"I can't afford one, I shall defend myself!" I told him. This threw them out of sync. and they stated that I would have to wait an extra hour or more to have my case heard.

Eventually I was called in by the officials and found that there was a witness against me who just happens to be the owner of the van involved. I'm questioned by a police officer who asks me where I was after the accident.

"I couldn't remember because I was suffering from concussion," I answered.

"Can you prove that statement is correct?"

"Yes, I went to the doctor's surgery and was signed off sick for three days," I replied.

The officials retire to discuss the case and after about an hour the court resumed. An announcement is made to the effect that the case is dismissed! Not guilty but not quite innocent, no fine and still no criminal record against me. Feeling relieved I am accosted by the same policeman.

"We will get you back for this," he stated.

I shrugged my shoulders and smirked, only to run into the owner of the van I damaged. It was apologies all round and we decided to have a drink in a pub in Reigate, just to show that there were no hard feelings.

When the neighbours and Monson Road club gossips found out about the outcome of my court case they were amazed with my nerve and cheek. It was talked about for quite a long time. No Surrey Mirror report on this issue this time. perhaps the police were too embarrassed! The police officer who uttered the "we will get you for this" was prophetic, because they did get a little bit of revenge which is part of my tale relating to my fourth brush with the law.

About five or six years after the car prang incident in the summer of 1974, a bizarre event took place. After an evening of drinking in some redhill pubs, the Wheatsheaf was usually the last point of call with friends and acquaintances. But this time the night was not over. Mick Sladkowski decided to open the doors of "The Baron's Nest", an upstairs steak house opposite the Tower pub. Mick could do this because his dad, Frank Sladkowski, was the proprietor of the Baron's Nest. It was a family run place with Mick's mum, his sister Linda and other relatives working as staff.

So, an impromptu party took place for the next couple of hours. other guests included Pam and her Bristow helicopter employee friends, Tony Wales, Mick's brother Stephen and three reprobates known only as "Tom, Dick and Harry". It was a crazy party, with dancing on the tables and lots of alcohol guzzling. But all good things come to an end and Mick decided to usher us all out and shut up shop. I was about to walk home, when a voice called out.

"Come on boys I'll give you a lift home"

It was Tony Wales who had his reliant three-wheeler in the car park behind the Tower. I got in the back and Steve Sladkowski was in the front passenger seat. Tony turned the ignition and was about to pull away when all of a sudden there were flashing blue lights and a siren blaring away. It was the Police !

Tony opened his door and ran off. Steve followed suit, both vanishing into the night. I was about to get out from the back when a policeman's boot stopped me from pushing the front seat down.

"You're not going anywhere" the officer said. Another policeman joins forces with the first one and between them they hoik me out of the Reliant. I get shoved into the back of a waiting police car and the driver swiftly pulls out of the car park, drives up London Road and then into Colesmead road. At the time I was thinking 'they're dropping me off home', but no. We moved along Southmead, up to Northmead and through to Gatton Park Road. By this time I'm beginning to feel pissed off! I spoke to the copper in the passenger seat.

"What are you playing at?" I asked.

"We're looking for the driver of the Reliant , Tony Wales," he answered in a harsh voice.

"Maybe if you speak to me in a more civil manner I'd try and help" I said. he replied in a more polite manner to previously

"Ok Mr Hall, where do you think we will find Mr. Wales" he said in a more polite manner than previously.

My response to this was simple.

" I don't know, and I don't fucking care"

The brakes were slammed on, shooting me forwards violently.

 "Ok sunshine back to the station and you can spend a bit of time in a cell to cool off " the offended copper says.

I'm driven back to the police station in Reigate and ushered to a cell.

"Is there a toilet in here? " I asked.

"There's a bucket you can piss in but don't do anything else," he replied.

Not exactly "five star" but I've soon fallen asleep on the rock-hard bed. A couple of hours later I'm woken up by a man in blue and ordered into the interview room. He stated that they have arrested Steve Sladkowski but still not found Tony Wales. He also said that Steve had been very stroppy and extremely rude. I replied that I couldn't blame him, because neither of us had committed a crime and if I was detained any longer, I would ask for a solicitor. The response to this was a nice cup of coffee and a lift home in the police car. I got out of the car in Colesmead rd. and then turned round to the Copper.

"Thanks for the lift but don't expect a tip !" I said.

When I walked indoors my mum was there.

"What have you been up to ?" she said in that severe way that only mothers can do!

"I'll tell you all about it later, I'm going to have a couple of hours sleep in a proper bed" I said. End of "brush with the law" number four and still no criminal record.

Six years after the Baron's Nest incident, a fifth brush with the law occurs. I was a victim of a crime that happened as I was delivering mail during my Post Office career. I was doing "London Road delivery", a pretty straight a forward round which started at London rd. shops and then progressed all the way up to Gatton Point petrol station, then back down the other side. With a few short roads and cul-de-sac along the way. One of my cushiest rounds!

However, I had got to Campion House at the bottom of Colesmead Rd. leaving my cycle propped against the wall of the flats. I took the bundle of letters from the mail bag and popped these into their respective doors on the ground, first and second floors. Then I went back downstairs. I came down to find the cycle in the same spot but with no bag on the rack. It had vanished! I had a walk about to see if a joke had been played on me and saw another postman in the Colesmead rd. area and asked him if had seen anything happen. No, he said, he'd seen nothing happen! There was nothing for it than to cycle back to the delivery office and report the theft of my mail bag and its contents. I was sent to the Investigations Branch. office to see Jack Steer, the man who was overseer of I.B. An interview took place and then police were called in, then another interview and questioning took place with a police officer. Both these people were very fair and respectful to me. I was then given other Post

Office duties to perform sorting and delivery preps. I found out sometime later that the contents of the mail bag had been strewn across the fields next to the road where the crime occurred. These fields were E.S.W. company property which also had a cricket ground and club for water company workers, situated along Frenches Road near the famous pond. All items of value such as cheques etc had been taken and the rest scattered all over the place. It sounds pretty tame, but this incident upset me and shook my confidence for a while. I was a conscientious postman and proud of the rapport I had with the public and my P.O. workmates.

I will finish this chapter with a statement about our police force, I have never been handcuffed or actually arrested or physically abused by any policeman, my only complaint is in the matter that they sometimes talk to you. By this I mean verbal abuse and a superiority complex as if they are speaking to an underling. Civility costs nothing and my experience as a postman taught me that is the best way of cooperation and rapport with the general public !

Chapter Five: Local Legends

I'll begin this chapter with a brief about the most famous crook in Redhill. I'm talking about Ronnie Biggs of course ! He lived in Alpine Road and I never knew or met him, but many of my workmates and relatives had worked with him and he was often seen in pubs around Redhill and Reigate. The great train robbery took place on the eighth of august 1963, which was also my sixteenth birthday. It was Ronnie's birthday as well although he was some years older at the time. When the Robbery happened, I was working at British Industrial Steel (B.I.S.). Many of my workmates and older friends claimed to have met him in local pubs and said that that he was not a bad bloke. I was jealous because I was still too young to go in a pub.

However, no matter what was said, Ronnie could not have been that nice a person as he was involved with petty crooks from London. There was also the fact that his father-in-law, a Reigate school headmaster, allegedly committed suicide due to his daughter Charmaine being involved with Biggs, who she eventually married. Biggs was not a leading player in the Robbery gang but became the most famous after his break-out from jail and his subsequent adventures around the world. This included giving his nemesis, Sergeant Slipper, the slip and eventually fathering a child with a Brazilian woman. There were of course numerous other events which have been well documented by the press and general media around the world, so I won't go into them here.

The aging lothario eventually came back to England to serve the remainder of his prison sentence until it was judged that he became too ill to finish it in jail. He was released and tended to by his faithful son, Michael, and died a sad and broken man.

I still think that the thirty-year sentence was too severe when you look at the awful crimes committed these days, with far less lenient punishments handed out. Certainly, the illegal actions undertaken now are worse than those done by the man from Alpine Road. He brought infamy to Redhill, and to this day I still don't have any admiration or respect for him, but at least he gave everyone something to talk about locally and further afield !

My next local legend is not actually local anymore as she moved to Outwood which is east of South Nutfield. Her husband was Michael Williams, a famous comedian of the time.

I am of course talking about an actress famous the world over, Dame Judy Dench. This esteemed personage was asked to officially open our brand-new callers office at the Redhill Post Office delivery depot which she duly accepted. It was scheduled for a midweek day during the nineties. between ten and eleven am. Judy was being escorted around our delivery office, with her guides explaining what went on in the workplace. I stayed out of the way, preferring to get on with preparing for my second delivery of the day. However, I could hear a crowd of 'posties', the managers, and Judy Dench chatting away. It went a bit quiet because Harry ('the cat knight' but we'll get to this later) was lining everyone up to take photos of everyone with Judy. All of a sudden, I could hear a female voice calling out:

"Rufus, Alan, Alan, get round here with Judy and us for the photos".

I wanted a quiet life and took no notice when suddenly I am approached by Judy, who puts her arm around me.

"Come on Alan, Cheryl wants you with us for our photos," she said.

The esteemed dame was so pleasant that I melted to her charm. 'What a lovely lady' I thought , as I walked around with her to join the rest of the jolly posties. The photos were taken by Harry, joined by other budding photographers. I still have a copy and compared to the rest of the crowd; I was not looking my best. But when you're standing next to Judy, Cheryl and other younger posties what do you expect !

I'll continue my tales with a tribute to the aforementioned, Harry 'The Cat Knight'. As you may have guessed from his title, Harry was well known for his love of cats. He kept three or four, sometimes even more in the yard outside the delivery office, just by the cycle sheds. Harry would feed and tend to them in between his duties as postman. The benefit of these felines here was to keep vermin away like mice and rats. We realised how well this worked well after he retired. With no one to look after then the cats were taken away. pest control people were brought in just weeks later,

Funds for the cats were raised by the Catman himself running a raffle each Friday. I was selling football cards at the same time to raise money for the football team I was playing for Johnstone Sports F.C. so there was a bit of competition. We never fell out over this but there was, lots of friendly banter. But nothing too catty !

Harry was married to the lovely Mary who shared his love of cats and I feel that maybe this compensated for the fact they never had any children. Harry came from Padstow in

Cornwall where he had driven steam trains. Before this he had been in the army, where he had competed in boxing and became a champion. If you met Harry, then you would never had realised this as he was just about the most mild mannered person you could ever meet.

He died some years ago and many attended his funeral along with me. The Redstone chapel was filled with people both inside and outside. So from being a Cornish train driver to a Redhill postman he certainly qualifies the title of a Redhill legend.

From an army boxing champion to a world middleweight boxing champion, Alan Minter who I met in the "Garland" pub in Redhill. One mid-week evening I was propped up by the bar with a pint of Best bitter in front of me, when in came two fellows that were not one of the familiar locals. I looked around to see if I recognised them and realised that the bigger fellow was Alan Minter. The other chap with him was swanning around.

"Do you know who this man is," he said, over and over again, like a silly court jester.

"Of course I know , who he is, sit down and make yourself scarce" I said.

Alan walks up to the bar next to me and orders drinks for him and the court jester. Alan had an orange juice due to the fact that he had an alcohol problem. I looked at Alan and was surprised at the size of him and the fact that he had an ominous aura. I spoke to him, asking him what he thought of the boxers fighting at the time, like Chris Eubank and Nigel Benn. We had a fairly long chat about the art of pugilism and then he stopped and pointed at the sweatshirt I was wearing. It was one of my real ale pub trail shirts.

 "You like your pub travels and real ale then" he said. We continued chatting about my pub adventures which he seemed quite interested in.

"I have a taxi coming to take us back to Reigate " the Court Jester said, walking up. Mr Minter held out his hand to shake mine and asked me my name.

"Same as yours, another Alan" I said.

The boxing champion and court jester departed for their taxi and then the landlord, Bill comes towards me and tells me off for keeping Minter talking for so long. Bill never really liked boxers.

"You narrow minded twat", I thought.

For those that do not know the history of Alan Minter, he was not world champion for long. He was cut to ribbons and destroyed by Marvin "Marvellous" Hagler! Alan minter died in 2021.

I'll continue this with a tale about a quartet of women who roamed the pubs of Redhill at the weekends. The Ladbroke Rd. ladies comprised of Winnie Copus, Chris Oakley, June Roberts and the fourth member I just can't remember! (perhaps there were only three with my memory playing tricks.)

Three of my five sisters - Lucy, Val and Iris, taken at the Toby Carvery (Lakers) by me. A celebration dinner for lucy's fiftieth birthday.

Winnie owned a house in Ladbroke Rd. with her husband. They kept lodgers and their postman was always busy with their police summons notices. Mr Copus sold evening newspapers in a box-style vendor in the middle of Redhill

Chris Oakley lived in the Ladbroke Cottages which were owned by the railway and rented to local train drivers which her husband Tom was. She was the mother of two lads. The oldest one, Terry, was a good friend of mine due to our mutual enjoyment of bar- billiards, football and cricket.

June Roberts had three sons, Barry, Andy and Phil, who I knew from my schooldays.

The Ladbroke Rd. ladies would begin their pub crawl at the Locomotive pub in Ladbroke Road itself. Many people would not venture in there because it was used by the local tough guys, labourers, roofers and building workers. I only went in there when I was a little older and more confident of myself.

Their next point of call would be the Southeastern opposite the railway station, whereas I mentioned in a previous chapter, Johnstone sports F.C began. This pub comprised of public and saloon bars and was actually an hotel which serve meals in the pub, a rare thing those days. Crisps, and pork pies with mustard were the normal order of the day in the sixties and early seventies.

When news of these ladies making their way to the Southeastern, some of the customers would scarper, and we are talking about so-called hard men here! these ladies would chat to all and sundry and were superb characters. They would drink and smoke just like the men, and why

not! From the southeastern " they would head to the
Wheatsheaf which was a favourite with the local Irish
community, I was in there one evening when all hell let
loose a local woman known as 'Motorway Rose' was there
mouthing off and rather foolishly upset Winnie Copus at
the same time. Winnie got up from her seat growling like a
bear, and heads towards Rose, who ran away to hide
behind the bar. The landlord 'Irish Martin" was having
none of it and cluttered off to the back room. Winnie went
behind the bar and grabbed hold of Rose. She punched
her in the back three or four times. All you could hear was
very scary screaming and growling coming from behind
the bar.

 If you don't know why 'Motorway Rose" was so called,
then I shall tell you. She used to entertain the navvies
working on the M25 section near North Merstham, where
they resided in temporary caravans. And of course we are
not talking about Vera Lynn style entertainment!

I will change tack now from human legends to a legendary
building, I am talking about the "Market Hall" in Station

Rd. which was razored down by the councillors of our posh neighbouring town of Reigate in the name of progress. This grand edifice was called the Market Hall and every Saturday we were entertained by many famous bands and local groups. Joe brown and his Brewers were one of the first I saw in this building, playing to a full house. My two older sisters were there too. Iris was wearing her distinctive spectacles and Val was sporting her brunette beehive hairstyle. Joe did his version of "Hava Nagila" playing the guitar on the back of his head. Classic stuff !

 Other famous groups played here. The Hollies visited at least three times and Allan Clark oiled his vocal chords with a couple of beers in the Tower pub. They were a superb band and one of my favourites for many years. We were entertained by other famous bands such as Johnny Kidd and the Pirates, the Searchers, Screaming Lord Sutch, Swinging Blue Jeans, Gerry and the pacemakers, Billy J Kramer and loads more.

These bands were preceded by local bands to warm the fans up and some were very talented. I will mention one band that cried off from playing here because they hit the top of the charts, Redhill was not cool enough for them !

They were called The Honeycombs" with a track called 'Have I the right' which went to number one at the top of the hit parade. They were mainly famous due to the fact that they had a female lead singer and a drummer who would thump away like mad ! But after time they were only known for producing that one hit wonders. I don't know if this was justice or not, but it still amuses me now. Ha bloody ha !

On a midweek evening well known jazz bands played in a smaller venue at the Market Hall. Traditional acts like Acker bilk and Kenny ball would play and many more lesser performers. My sister Val and my Uncle Jim often went to these concerts. I never went because I preferred rock and blues music but it was also due to the fact that I was invariably skint by mid-week! Having said that I did like Acker Bilk's 'Stranger on the shore' and Kenny Ball's, 'Midnight in Moscow'.

I will move from this iconic building to a person known by many residents of Redhill and beyond. His name is Dave

Hunt who compared to me is almost as big as a building. He's six foot eight with a huge frame. I first knew Dave from working at B.I.S. in January 1963. He was the largest person I had ever met and I must have been the smallest at fifteen and a half years old. At that time I was just four foot eleven inches tall (or short) and six and a half stone in weight. The original 'Little and Large' for those that remember them. Prior to working at B.I.S., Dave was conscripted into the army and he joined the grenadier guards along with his elder brother, Reg. His wife Marian has told me that his large size and dark skin was due to his ancestors being of Canadian Cree descent. Dave left B.I.S to work at the Post Office which I also joined in in 1972. He had to have a delivery bicycle custom made with two crossbars to hold his weight. I would have needed a step ladder to get on that and it would look like I was riding a Penny Farthing !

Dave and Marion hunt at Redhill bus station. another of my first workmates at B.I.S, my lifelong friend and we still chat regularly on the phone.

Dave was a Redhill and district football referee in the sixties and seventies. His decisions were final, as no one would argue with him ! I remember when Steve Williams, commonly known as Wilbur tried to wind him up on the pitch when playing for the team 'Merstham Newton'.

"How long have we got dummy ?" he asked the referee.

Dave looked at his watch.

"Twelve minutes but for you sonny; None, your off" said the big man giving him the red card. That would teach him to be so gobby!

Dave was the first to congratulate me after I had a set to with Charley Bone, an ominous man who lived in Merstham but was originally an Eastender from London. For some reason he hated me and was quite abusive. The fight went well and I managed to land half a dozen punches without him hitting me. Charley was led away to clean his blood off his face. I was actually shaking with fear, but this had turned into aggression. A Bit of self-defence!

Sometime after this we became friends due to Dave's persuasions. I found out from Charlie as to why he was quite bitter with life. it was down to his time in World War Two where he came home as the sole survivor of his troop. He had lost all his friends which is enough to make anybody bitter.

Dave is an excellent crossword solver, and we would often sit in the P.6, canteen poring over the newspaper's crosswords. he has won many prizes from the Radio Times and major broad- sheet papers and he is still doing them now at the age of 84. We went to many football matches together and Merstham F.C was always his first choice. At home matches Dave would be in the club shop selling the team's merchandise. We both collected football club badges and made many special trips to add to our collections. So Dave was well known for his many years delivering the local mail, his refereeing career and his charismatic presence. The definition of a local legend !

I will conclude this chapter with à smattering of different pub characters. The first person is Harry Weller. a big, rounded fellow, shaped like a bear. The Sultan was his favourite pub where he challenged all and sundry to games of darts. A pint or a pound would be at stake, and he was victorious in many games. After he threw a winning dart, he would shout "'ang your 'at"(hang your hat). His life came to a sad end after an evening in the Anchor pub. Walking home up Grove Hill Road toward his lodgings after, he fell down a hole that had been dug for gas workings. Harry was found dead next morning from a heart attack brought on by hypothermia caused by being in the hole all night. A very sad end to a popular Redhill man.

The next pub character is Charlie Brazil, an Earlswood man. The Sultan was also his favourite pub. The Landlord, Fred Cooper, often hired a pianist to entertain his customers at weekends and ti was so popular that he had difficulty in getting rid of his punters at end of evenings. Fred got round this by asking Charlie to sing some songs. His voice was so awful and loud that it did the trick. after most of them had gone Fred would stop the music saying that he had a migraine coming on. Social night at the Sultan was over !

Michael More" known as "Irish Mick" was well known around the pubs. He came to Redhill to work on the M25 but stayed on to work as a ganger for companies doing road excavations. Mick must have liked our pubs and women; he married one and had a daughter with her. In his retirement years Mick spent many an hour in the Redhill's Wetherspoon pub, The Sun. He would talk to all and sundry over a pint of Guiness including myself. Mike spoke of his tough life in Ireland before coming to Redhill. He was the same age as me, and his birthday was three weeks after mine. So in August we would treat each other to a pint of Guinness.

 Michael sadly died this year - January 2022. R.I.P. you jolly old Irishman!

From an Irishman to a Welshman called, believe it or not, Taffy. I don't know his actual name and I never heard any one address him as anything but Taffy. He was a typical no-nonsense Welshman, worked as a roof tiler and was tough as old boots. He was loud and his speech was peppered with swear words. Taffy was self-employed and one of his co-workers was Pete Gunner another gritty Colesmead man. Peter had a nasty accident working with Taffy. He fell off a roof and suffered brain damage. What brain he had left, after all the years of beer, sherry and spirits had pretty much sozzled it. However, Taffy and his wife took him in as a lodger and looked after Pete until he died a couple of years later. So Taff was tough but with a good heart

I can remember chatting with Taff in the Sun pub one evening about world cup football. England were to play Wales the next day.

"How about a bet then ?" Taffy asked.

"I don't gamble as a rule" I replied.

"Put your money where your mouth is."

""What's the stake ?"

"A pint" Taff said.

"You're on !" I agreed.

England did beat Wales despite having the great Gareth Bale on their side. I didn't see Taffy for some time after this but eventually he made an appearance in the Sun" I said to him

" Have you welshed on your bet?" I said.

Taff looked at me for a while realising what I was talking about then fished out a fiver.

"Get yourself a fucking pint" he said. Cheers Taff!

He ended up wheelchair-bound due to emphysema. But even then Taff would crash through the doors of the Sun in his typical aggressive manner. He died about three years ago and the Sun hosted a wake for him. It was packed with family and his many friends. To this short pugnacious and popular Welshman, I say R.I.P. you left your mark !

Another of our reunions in the Sun pub. (Left to Right) Ronnie Lambert, Micky Sladkowski and Steve Jones.

I will finish off this part about legends with a round- up of the local gangs at the time. I've already mentioned the McBride family, they were not to be messed and even their sisters were scary. Next up were the McCarthy family. most of these were scary, the weakest link being Jim. He lived off the reputation of his older family and often came off second best in punch ups! I have some history with him.

Then you had the Smith brothers, who came from Ireland to find work down here and were industrious chaps. They spent many an hour in our pubs especially the Locomotive and the Southeastern. They were usually quite agreeable lads and their fighting tended to be against each other more than anyone else. I saw them scrapping with each other in the car park next to the Southeastern a couple of times.

 There was also the Lambert Brothers. These guys were always friendly. the 'Dodimeads' were well known in the pubs and were very popular. The youngest was George who was known as "medallion man". He had jewellery around his neck and his wrists with rings on all his fingers. He would put "Del boy" to shame. There was an assortment of gangs from Merstham, Horley, Reigate,

Woodhatch and even Bletchingley. There were many territorial fights including the seaside battles between mods and rockers. The music these warriors fought over was created in the sixties and fifties respectively. Then in the early seventies after we got punk music (music ?). It was enough to drive you to classical music, which was the case for me ! Then the Eighties came and along with it were the sickly yuppies who couldn't fight their way out of paper bags, so the use of knives came into play. My own brother Pat was a victim of stabbing and was in hospital for some time but thankfully he made a full a recovery. And to this day he is my favourite brother and my best friend, so I'll conclude this chapter on that happy note.

08

Chapter five: Musical Dalliances.

My first experience of music was listening to the radio in particular the BBC light programme channel. Family Favourites on Sundays was exactly that in our living room in Colesmead and we would cheer if one of our favourite records were played. During the fifties there were solo artistes like Elvis Presley, Ricky Nelson, Brenda Lee but there were not so many bands in those days. There was but we had Lonnie Donegon and his skiffle band. We also used to listen to Tommy Steele, Acker Bilk and Kenny Ball.

During the evenings we would tune in to Radio Luxembourg. They would play more up-to-date records than the stuffy old BBC. The only problem was that "Radio Lux" had a habit of fading away for moments and coming back even louder. You would sometimes also get hideous whistling noises, a novel way to share my tinnitus with the rest of the family.

When money became less tight, we had a Radiogramme which consisted of a record player with four different speed: 16, 33, 45 and 78 r.pm. This player was sat on top of the radio. I think our first records were Joe Brown's "Picture of you", a golden guinea LP, (my sister Iris'). The first '45' record we had was Val's. The A-side was "It's late" by Ricky Nelson with "My bucket's got a hole in it" on the B-side. I remember our dad hated the "bucket" song.

During these times the BBC had a restrictive "needle time" imposed on them. The recording companies wielded more power in those days. Then in the sixties a big change came in the form of radio pirate ships. One of which was Radio Caroline. Tony Blackburn and Kenny Everett, amongst others, were the pirate DJ's . This was eventually outlawed and the BBC was transformed and modernised with more local channels.

Even this became slightly old-hat with the DAB radio system coming into our lives with their ever growing and multi-national stations covering all kinds of music, religious, DIY and gay channels. Something for everyone!

Back in the fifties and sixties people used to entertain themselves more, sometimes by playing instruments.

Everything from harmonicas and accordions to guitars. And if they couldn't play an instrument they could always sing. They would do this in their own homes or clubs and pubs.

My dad used to play the harmonica, the accordion and sometimes the spoons. Occasionally he would even sing. My grandad was also a very good accordion player. My mum, not to be left out, was often called on to sing at the Monson Rd. club. Vera Lynn songs was one of her favourites, along with Connie Francis. Nellie coombes was another guest singer who favoured Judy Garland songs. other guest singers were Jimmy Egan, Claire Pemble and Alun Thomas. There was also a chimney sweep from Frenches Road who sung operatic songs, pulling all sorts of contorted faces in the process. I also played the mouth organ quite regularly and for a short while I compered the acts on Saturday nights. I am pleased to say this didn't last too long because as a social committee member also had to do the bingo nights which sometimes got in the way.

One Sunday night whilst calling the numbers I happened to say something funny or maybe crazy which sent the bingo players into hysterical laughter for about fifteen minutes. That brought to an end my compering and bingo caring duties. This was bliss, as I could concentrate on playing the harmonica. My first mouth organ was a birthday present from my dad as I had begged him to get me my own. I think I was ten and the instrument was probably bought from a shop called Rhythms situated at Station Road in Redhill. They sold all kinds of instruments, song sheets, and of course records. Many an hour was spent in this shop, browsing through the discs on offer. Although half the time I couldn't afford to buy anyway. After thanking dad for my birthday present, I asked him if he could teach me to play it. He replied politely that it was not possible, that you had to just practice on your own until you hit some of the right notes and eventually combine them until you got a song right. The first tune that I managed was 'God save the queen', our national anthem. I learned it because in those days pretty much everyone was a royalist. At least I think they were. Next up

I learned some Irish and Scots folk songs. Then I branched out trying the American country music. From there I managed to play Bob Dylan's blowing in the wind" and the aptly named 'Puppet on a string. Barefoot Sandy Shaw's Eurovision song. Then came Elvis's G.I Blues song 'Wooden Heart' which I often played as a duet with my dad.

When I felt the confidence to play in front of an audience, I would take the harmonica to school (Frenches secondary) to entertain my school mates in the playground during class breaks. Although I would get quizzical looks from some of the teachers as I didn't exactly shine in music lessons. The teacher that we had for those was Mr. Nuttall. He was pretty cantankerous and just about the crappiest pianist I ever heard. Although I mostly didn't enjoy his lessons as he was a religious education teacher as well, so consequently the music lesson normally consisted of singing hymns. Not my cup of tea !

After leaving school my new audience was my workmates. When I was old enough (or nearly old enough)

I started going to clubs. In particular the Monson Rd club and the British Legion" in Redhill and also various pubs. Here I occasionally played with pianists and organ players. Often there were outings to the seaside such as the one organised by the Darts club. This was another chance for everyone to sing and play their instruments. One time we stopped off at a social club in Dagenham. There we were all invited to sing or play a turn during the evening until the resident pianist took their break. Lofty Chapman took over as compere as he liked the sound of his own voice. In a change of pace, he came up with the novel idea of inviting people to tell jokes on stage. When it came to my turn, I had to rack my brain to come up with something short and not so sweet:

"Have you heard the one about the bloke who went to redhill public lavatories with a bent penny?"

"No," said the audience back to me.

"He shit himself," I said.

There were gasps all round and I was promptly escorted off the stage by Lofty Chapman.

So along with my bingo antics, my joke telling career was over, as quick as it started. (To be honest it was one of my dad's jokes. He is definitely where I got my gritty sense of humour from.)

When I was about 17 had a week's holiday at Butlins in Bognor Regis with an old schoolmate named Paul. By Monday I was getting a bit bored with stuff like boating lakes, fairground rides and the rest of the razzamattaz and went for a walk. As I strolled through the holiday camp, I noticed one of the theatres asking for volunteers to take part in their weekly talent contests. So that afternoon I walked in and registered me to perform with my harmonica. I played "Wooden heart", one of my favourite songs. Every afternoon from the first Monday until the finals on Friday I played it. But that evening, as they say in horse racing, I was an also ran. I was obviously not going to be the Larry Adler of Redhill. (I also got fed up playing the same tune every day. Excuses, excuses !).

Another memory which stands out in my mind is when I had my first overseas holiday. I was about twenty-six years old and our choice was Benidorm, Spain's most famous holiday resort at the time. the other guys that went with me were Mick and Steve Sladkowski and the Brazil brothers, Ian and Bob. (Mick and I are, at the time of writing, the only two still alive out of this team) My trusty mouth organ was with me as always and I sometimes played in the hotel gardens by the swimming pool. The hotel lounges had entertainment of different sorts but on the Friday's and Saturday's the local band took to the stage. I was invited to join them and I was a bit reluctant at first, with my recent Butlins also-ran performance still fixed in my mind. I eventually agreed to play with the band on Saturday evening. Although I was a bit scruffy, so the head waiter lent me his very smart shirt for my big moment. I took nervous sip of a drink to calm me down just before I was called up to the stage to play. As I walked up, I was urged on and cheered by my holiday mates and other hotel guests. I seemed to have an instant rapport with this Spanish band and played my usual repertoire, however one of the musicians asked if I could play 'When the saints go marching in'. I told them that I'd give it a go. My efforts went down really well as we seemed to have a great unity between us. I made that my final tune as then I could leave the stage with the self-satisfaction of a job well done and some nice applause.

Playing my harmonica on a hotel stage with a local Spanish band at Benidorm.

The label from a bottle of beer specially done for me on my seventieth birthday by Pat and Sharon. How cool is that!

I got rather drunk that night with the rest of our gang and the next morning was woken up in my hotel room with a rata-tat on the door. It was the head-waiter asking for his shirt back which I duly gave him. I thanked him again and apologised that it was steeped in sweat. (Spain in mid-summer was bloody hot !) I carried on playing the harmonica until 1997, just beyond my 50th birthday which I celebrated with a party in the Greyhound pub in Brighton Road. I hired a disco which was DJ'ed by Colin Wales and there was good spread of food out on the tables. Dave and Liz Stacey were running the pub in those days and they did me proud , a really a nice couple.

Sharon and Pat on his fiftieth birthday with a glass of Guiness, born on St. Patrick's day

However, a week before Christmas at the Post Office where I worked, I ate some cookies that someone had brought in. But unbeknownst to me they were laced with drugs. I had an adverse effect to these and I was rushed to hospital with a slight stroke. This eventually led to my early retirement in September of 2002. Sometime after the "cookie incident" , I thought I'd have a practice on my mouth organ. To my dismay the co-ordination which I used to have was gone and I just couldn't string a tune together any more. I guess that was the end of my playing days !

After this I developed an interest in American country music as performed by the likes of Hank Williams, Slim Whitman and Johnny Cash. I especially had a fondness for the yodellers and after listening to CD's of these artistes I started having a go at this myself. I practised indoors trying different yodelling songs but it was a while before I had the confidence to do this in local pubs. But when I did the pub customers were amused but seemed to be approve all the same.

 Recently (early 2022), the Garibaldi pub in Redhill put on Karaoke on a Saturday night (but they called it 'Garioki',

Ho Ho !) I was asked to do a turn, so I thought "yeah give it a go". Up until then I was always a bit 'anti-karaoke. I decided to sing Bob Dylan's " blowing in the wind", as I said, one of one of my favourite harmonica tunes. To start with I messed up and the guy controlling the karaoke equipment stopped and asked me to start again. So I turned round and said "ok, it's take | two" and then burst into song. During the harmonica parts I mimed as if I was playing it (wishful thinking!). At the end I was given some applause at least as much as everyone else did at the end of their turns. So, I say to anyone, if you feel you have something to offer musically just go for it ! You could be the next Elvis, opera singer or Eric Clapton. Who incidentally was raised in Surrey. Just like yours truly !

Chapter Six: Mishaps and Ailments

I've already mentioned having pneumonia at the turn of my first birthday. So, I'll swiftly move on to when I was twelve and a half years old . My doctor, Watson by name, deemed it necessary for me to have my tonsils and adenoids surgically removed. This operation took place at East Surrey Hospital in Shrewsbury Road. People used to say that this procedure was straightforward and almost painless, it was anything but. I was placed in a bed in the men's surgical ward. I was not a child nor a man but racing towards my teen years. I was ordered to fast for twenty four hours, so all I was allowed was sips of water and milk. When the time came round for my operation my stomach was rumbling and was feeling pretty weak. A nurse came to see me armed with a needle and syringe. I was ordered to lay on my stomach.

"This won't hurt," she said, as she pulled my pyjama trousers down and jabbed me in the bum. It did bloody well hurt. After this I was wheeled into the operating theatre. It was not stage-fright but absolute terror that I felt. I was laid on my back with Dr. Watson hovering over me with his nurses. A gas mask was placed over my mouth and I was told to count to ten. I got to four and I was out.

 I woke up the next morning with my throat raging with pain and occasionally being sick. As soon as I started throwing up, the nurses swished the curtains around my bed, making me feel like some kind of leper, (unclean, unclean!) Saying that though, the staff were all friendly and sympathetic, including two Jamaican nurses who were always chatting and laughing. The rest of the patients were just as caring. Barry, a seventeen-year-old, was in the next bed to me and was the second youngest apart from me in the ward. Appendicitis was his problem and he showed me his scar on his stomach which looked absolutely horrific. Also, each bed area was equipped with a radio headphone, so I could listen to the latest pop songs. A luxury that I never expected to have, so all in all it was not all doom and gloom!

I was in the hospital for six days before I was considered well enough to be discharged. Mum came to take me home and we walked into town to catch a bus to Colesmead road as we could not afford taxis in those days. This happened at the start of the decade that would become the swinging sixties. About a week later I was taken to see Dr. Watson for a general check-up.

"Is he fit enough to go to school?" asked my mum.

"You can do what you like with him," the Doctor replied.

"Back to school tomorrow my boy" was mum's reaction to that.

So back to school it was and my classmates were asking me where I had been the last couple of weeks. I told them about my operation and they said I was a lucky boy to have two weeks off school. I think I'd rather be taking lessons than lying around in a hospital bed!

The next incident came about after leaving school when I was working for B.I.S Ltd. I was about sixteen and had joined Merstham youth club in Radstock way. I made many friends here and was made very welcome by the Merstham estate clan. One evening I overstepped the mark a little. I got talking to Dave Jones who was into boxing training with his brothers and mates.

"There was someone like you at the Co-op yesterday," I said.

 "What do you mean?" Dave said.

"They had a chimp doing an advertising stunt," I answered.

Understandably Dave was rather angry. I tried to apologise and back-track, but the damage was done.

"I'll see you outside and sort you out," he said.

 Later when I left to catch the bus home, I heard my name being called. I turned to see Dave walking towards me.

"I didn't like what you said in there" he said and before I could say anything he slammed three punches into my face. I walked away to the bus stop and realised that blood was oozing from my nose. Two of Dave's mates caught up with me and asked if I was alright. I told them that I would be once the bus took me back home. They turned round and gave Dave a good telling off. I got home and went straight to bed somewhat ashamed of myself for getting into such a silly predicament.

After this I stuck to Redhill for my entertainments. I was in town one Saturday afternoon when I spotted Dave Jones walking towards me.

"What the bloody hell is he gonna do now," I thought to myself'

As he walked toward me, Dave offered his hand for me to shake. He apologised saying that he felt really bad about the whole thing. We did shake hands and had a chat, both of us realising how silly we had been.

"Can we be friends now ?" Dave asked.

"Yes of course," I said.

And to this day we have been the best of mates. Dave has become one of the recognised characters of Merstham and Redhill and beyond. He was well known as the owner of a three- legged dog who went everywhere with him, on buses and into the pubs. I think the canine tripod became more famous than Dave! The dog eventually died and Dave reluctantly took on another one. This one was a similar size and shape but blessed with four legs. The new dog has his own stamp of personality just like Dave and goes everywhere with him.

From the age of sixteen until my mid-twenties, I stayed quite fit and healthy and generally incident-free with no more accidents or scraps (at least I don't think there were?). Just under a year of working at the post office and December came.

And with it came the Christmas pressure.

In order to keep up with the demand we had to work twelve hours on and then had twelve hours off. Stretching from Monday to Saturday plus Sunday morning duties. This lasted for three and a half weeks, so by then end of the Christmas and New year period, postman Alan was pretty knackered!

On the upside lots of drinking took place, and New Year's Eve was celebrated in drinking establishments such as the Brickmakers, Gatton point and the Monson rd. club. After seeing in the new year at the club I went home to bed to sleep it all off. But on waking up on New Year's Day morning, I felt absolutely awful but went to the toilet and got back to bed.

"Are you getting up, there's jobs to do," said Mum, checking in on me later.

"I think I've got flu," I said weakly. She studied my face.

"I think, you're right, you look awful. Would you like a cup of tea ?",

I nodded a feeble "yes please" but after a few sips of my tea and I nodded off again. I was languishing like for two or three days but eventually recovered and went back to work about five days later. For a couple of weeks or so I was still quite weak and tired, making work a bit of an ordeal. A lot of people say that having flu is like a heavy cold. It is definitely not. It is debilitating and can kill you. For many years now I've had the flu jab in the autumn, and I fail to understand why many people do not. I think they like to be anti-everything just to be different. Get real!

A couple of years after the flu experience I had a minor accident indoors. I had woken up about two in the morning to relieve my bladder of the last night's beer intake. I walked into the toilet and closed the door.

Suddenly I slipped over, due to the lino being covered in water. My head crashed against the side of the bath. I swore and pulled myself back up onto my feet and did what I had originally come to do. With an aching head, I staggered back to bed and promptly fell straight asleep.

On waking up and seeing the clock, I realised I was a bit late for work at the Post office I had a shocking headache and when I looked in the mirror could see that I had a swollen face and a cut across my right ear. I made myself a cup of tea and decided that I was not in a fit state to work. With that in mind I walked to the hospital (in Pendleton Road). It was quite a walk, but I was still young and pretty fit in those days. I walked into A & E and was attended to quickly. I had six surgical stitches in the ear and pain killers to ease my aching head. I was signed off sick from work for a week, (which was a nice little rest), and the stitches in my ear were taken out at the doctor's surgery five days later. During which I'm told that I have a fractured cheek bone alongside my right ear. I asked what can be done about that and the doctor said it will heal of its own accord.

Oh, the magic of medicine! A week after this mishap I returned to work with a scar on my ear and my head swelling gradually diminishing.

As I have said, I worked as a welder in the sixties and early seventies.to my welding days. Most of my work was with steel which required me to do electric arc-welding. I also did gas welding on copper and aluminium, plus the oxyacetylene steel cutting flame machine. The electric grinder I also used quite a lot to smooth over any lumps and bumps. These machines were quite scary instruments to use, especially for a scrawny teenager like myself. So, I had to toughen up quite quickly ! They all had their risks, but the electric arc was the most dangerous because it created a bright, hot, flashing light, which meant you had to have screens around you while this work took place to protect others. However, you sometimes got caught unawares and when this happened you could get damage to your vision known as arc-eye. This would not be immediately apparent, and it would take a few hours for you to feel the effects. By mid-evening you would start to get itchy eyes, as if you had sand or grit thrown in your eyes. The glare of sunlight made it quite painful as well, so dark sunglasses were needed. But you could get some relief by covering your eyes with damp teabags. This affliction could last up to three days. I had this happen to me at least three or four times so all in all it was a blessing in disguise when my welding career came to an end in late 1971. The industry was failing anyway, aided "by 'sailor'

Ted Heath's mismanaging government. Then the 4-day week and the power cuts to thwart the miner made things worse. The miners were eventually finished off by the "Iron lady"(How ironic, if you'll pardon the pun).

When I was about 58 years old, I had polyps in the bowel surgically cut out. I won't bore you with the details of this procedure, but I could see what was going on via looking a bedside camera while the doctor explained what was happening. Just looking at this made me feel quite sick.

I'd like to move on to February 2017 when a bizarre incident took place. There was snow and ice all around and I risked my neck walking down to Sainsbury's in town. I'd started putting food and items in a shopping basket when my nose started to drip. I had a cold, so I put a handkerchief to it and soon realized my nose was bleeding. After a while it still had not stopped, so I spoke to my brother, Pat, who was working in Sainsbury at the time, stacking shelves and so on. Pat told me to sit at the side of the shop and that he would fetch me a member of staff who was a first aider. He came over to me and tried to stop the blood flow but after a while he gave up and called the hospital. An ambulance turned up, but they didn't have any success either. They took me to the hospital and was taken into A&E. I had to wait a while till an ear, nose and throat specialist was called to examine me. As that Doctor could also not staunch the bleeding so he decided to take drastic action. I thought he was going to punch me on the nose, but he was a complete gentleman. He explained that he was going to push a surgical instrument up into my nostril and through to the inside of my head.

"This will hurt," he said.

"It's got to be better than dying from blood loss," I said.

"Are you ready," he asked, by but by this time I was past caring. The instrument the doctor rammed into my nose looked like the middle of a dart, the weight part or maybe a fisherman's flight. He was right, it did hurt and he secured the thing by tying bandages around the back of my head. The he informs me that I had to stay in hospital for some time and that the staff will find a bed for me. I was eventually placed in a ward which dealt with blood complications. I was stuck in hospital from Thursday until Sunday evening and I felt like a caged animal. I whiled away the time in hospital by acting as a paperboy and librarian.

Pat and Sharon picked me up and took me home as there was still lots of snow and ice all around. After this awful time, I never (touchwood) had any more trouble with really nose bleeds. But I still suffered for many years with this problem which would be triggered off by hot weather, sneezing, and sometimes after having a beer or two.

From the age of sixty I became the proud owner of a bus pass. to start with this was only county wide, but from 2008 became nation-wide. This was big news across the world, even Australia where my friend, Ian piddock was living and working. However, one Thursday afternoon I took a trip to Epsom with Keith Jordan (known as the long man), on the 460 bus. It was quite a scenic route through Walton-on-the hill etc. The bus driver seemed to be in a hurry as it was running late. I am on the top deck reading my daily mirror as we were approaching Epsom downs racecourse when all of a sudden, the bus started lurching and shaking about like mad. It came to a stop after this. Due to the mayhem, the passengers were screaming, shouting and swearing at the driver. I looked outside the window to see that we had actually ended up on the grass of the famous Epsom racecourse. Eventually police cars and ambulances arrived, and one by one we were all escorted off the bus which was at a dangerous and jaunty angle. All the passengers were taken to an onsite builders' canteen and office (some work was being carried out on the course). We were given seats and offered drinks, tea, coffee and water, that sort of thing. After this the medical staff took our names and addresses, asking us if we had any injuries and so on. Some of the passengers were taken to hospital with slight bruises and cuts. Keith and I were somewhat shaken up but otherwise we were all in one piece. So, we were O.K.'d by the medical staff to leave and get another bus into Epsom town.

We decided to go to a Wetherspoons pub, the Assembly Rooms to enjoy a curry and a couple of beers. We took our seats and chose from the menu. I got up to order at the bar and then remembered that I needed the table-number. I looked at Keith and he had a strange look on his face.

"What is it? " I asked.

Keith pointed at the number.

"It's thirteen," he said.

"Shall we move to another table?" I asked.

"It's a bit late now we've had our accident for the day" Keith replied.

After curry and beers were consumed, we went back home (nervously) on the 460 bus. That evening I popped into the Garland pub for a beer, served by Leslie, Stuart's lovely wife.

"What's wrong with your face?" Leslie asked.

"What do you mean?" I said.

"It looks all pinky!"

I told her about the accident on the bus to Epsom, and she said that I must be suffering from shock"

Yes, it was a nasty shock, and we got over it, just in time for the next one!

On Saturday 5th May 2018, I went to the Oval at Kennington to watch Surrey versus Worcestershire with "the Captain" (John). We watched the cricket from about 2pm until 5pm when we decided it was time for a few beers, like you do on a Saturday evening. Walking out of the Oval we started to walk across the first slip road after checking it was all clear. I got halfway across this road when I noticed this black car cutting across the right-hand lane of the main road. Suddenly it zoomed into the slip road where John and I were crossing. I looked across to see the bonnet of the car hurtling toward me at great speed, and thought my number was up. But instinctively I managed to scamper a few feet, but the side of the car still caught me. My body seemed to circle around the side of the motor as it sped past. I ended flat on my back in the middle of the road. The car just carried on at the same speed and then disappeared from sight. John was on the pavement on the other side of the road looking dazed and confused. Then this fellow was standing over me.

"Are you alright?" he asked.

"If you give me a hand up, I shall see" I said.

He helped me up and I thought I felt ok. As I walked to the safety of the pavement, I noticed I was bleeding from my left wrist. I stuck an Elastoplast over the cut and then I noticed that my left forearm was swelling up. With that, we carried on towards Vauxhall rail station and got a train to East Croydon. There we went to Cronks bar around the corner from the station. We had a couple of beers here, and I asked the barman for some ice cubes to rub across my left arm which was aching quite a bit by this time. From there we made our way to the George in Croydon, we met Jeff and Marylin in here and also Ian piddock arrived. I told them all about my accident and they all agreed that I was lucky not to be seriously injured. The next day my hip was aching but apart from that I seemed o.k. and I went to Sainsbury's for my Sunday shop, where I met Mike Sladkowski. I told him about my accident.

"Al, your voice has gone all croaky," he said ",it must be shock."

I recovered from this and think to myself that I am lucky to still be alive. I think I have used all my nine lives up.

After all I am a Leo!

Epilogue

Over the years I've had people say to me "I hate Redhill, I'd like to leave." My response has always been "Well what's stopping you?" The sort of feeble answers I hear to this question are:

"I can't afford to move; I'd have to change my job" or "my wife won't move away." Oh dear!

I know the town is a mess, thanks. to the meddling councillors from Reigate and Banstead, but Redhill is not just about the town. We have lost many superb buildings like the Market Hall and the Odeon cinema, both in station road. Also, the Colman institute, which housed the library where I borrowed many books during my childhood and beyond. The Co-op store was prominent where you could buy practically everything you could think of in London Road, along with the Sultan pub, which Fred Cooper and wife Nellie presided over. Many other buildings have been razored down in the name of so-called progress. However, on the outskirts of the town, there are many pleasant areas. Near where I live you have Mill Street, opposite Redhill common and the superbly run Garibaldi pub. Further down you have the Plough with St. John's church in the background. you have Reffells bridge where the Red Lion sits, and Redstone hill which our town gets its name from. It houses the Home Cottage pub and the Toby Carvery.

The A25 road leads through to Nutfield, Bletchingley and Godstone green. All worthy of a visit. If you feel the need to get away from Redhill it could not be any easier. The bus services are good. The rail station is a junction which can transport you to Reading and the southwest. Or to the north you have London and to the east, the whole of Kent beckons. To the south of course, the whole of Sussex and its coastlines.

On top of that you have Gatwick airport to take you anywhere in the world, many of my travels have been from there. There are many interesting and quirky characters in Redhill and I have made many friends over the years. Many people have come to work here and settled. Some of which were Irish, Welsh, Scottish, Indian and Pakistani. People from all over the world have swelled our ranks, and I feel it makes Redhill a very interesting place to live.

So, to conclude this book, I say to you, if you don't like Redhill you can slope off to somewhere else where you may also be just as discontented and unpopular as you were before.

Cheers everyone !

Acknowledgements

I have been overwhelmed by the support and encouragement that I've been given by so many people. From my siblings, nephews, and nieces alike, to the many people I drink and socialise with in the pubs in and around Redhill. Thanks to Colin Wales and Micky Sladkowski and others for helping to fill in some gaps and dates. They both get honourable mentions in my tales.

Halfway into writing this i lost my sister iris. As low a time in my life, I can't think of. I don't think she was aware of this project as she was suffering from her illness so much. I'm sure she will be smiling down on me!

And lastly but not least, I cannot thank Paul Lister enough for working and assisting on this book. His unwavering support has been amazing with his infectious humour and charm when we were at the Home Cottage pub garden, where he wrote his own books on those literary lawns. And thanks to the staff of this pub for their attentive attitude, bringing our beers out to the garden to Paul and myself.

Many thanks everyone and cheers!

 Alan Hall

Printed in Great Britain
by Amazon